Good Sports

Winning. Losing.
And Everything in Between

By Therese Kauchak

Illustrated by Norm Bendell

AmericanGirl™

Published by Pleasant Company
Publications
For information, address: American Girl
Library Editor, Pleasant Company
Publications, 8400 Fairway Place,
P.O. Box 620998, Middleton, WI 53562.

Visit our Web site:
www.americangirl.com

Printed in the United States of America.
99 00 01 02 03 04 WCR 10 9 8 7 6 5 4 3 2 1
American Girl Library® is a registered
trademark of Pleasant Company.

Editorial Development: Michelle Watkins
Art Direction: Kym Abrams
Design: Karen Gibson
Cover Photography: Jim Jordan
Interior Photography: Will van Overbeek
Historical Photo Credits: Brown Brothers,
Culver photos
Book Production: Janette Sowinski,
Richmond Powers

Special thanks to:
Mary Jo Kane, Tucker Center for
Research on Girls and Women in Sports
Russell Pate, Department of Exercise
Science, University of South Carolina
Jody Lavin Patrick

Library of Congress Cataloging-in-
Publication Data
Kauchak, Therese, 1964
Good sports: winning, losing, and every-
thing in between / by Therese Kauchak ;
illustrated by Norm Bendell. — 1st ed.
p. cm.
"American girl library."
Summary: Provides advice on being a
great teammate and a good winner, tips
on keeping the mind and body strong, plus
advice from professional women athletes.
ISBN 1-56247-747-1
1. Sportsmanship Juvenile literature.
2. Sports for children—Social aspects—
United States Juvenile literature.
[1. Sportsmanship.] I. Bendell, Norm, ill.
II. American girl (Middleton, Wis.)
III. Title.
GV706.3 .K38 1999 796–dc21
99-29202 CIP

Dear Reader,

Here's your own personal playbook designed to help you be the best athlete you can be. Inside you'll find tips on being a great team player. You'll get advice on keeping your body—and mind—strong. Quizzes reveal if you're a good winner and a good loser. Plus, fun drills and secrets from sports stars help improve your skills. There are even memory pages where you can record your dreams and goals, and sports moments you'll never forget. But want to know the biggest sports secret of all? You should play to have fun. So go to it!

Your friends at American Girl

Lineup

warming
Up

Girls in sports **stand tall.**

Go Play!

When it comes to playing sports today, your choices seem endless. But that hasn't always been the case. For centuries, women of all ages were warned against participating in strenuous physical activities. They'd faint, people said, or injure themselves, or maybe even hurt their chances of having children someday. Of course, in reality, women had been doing all kinds of strenuous work around the house, farm, or factory for years.

By the late 1800s, though, women took part in more enjoyable forms of physical activity. School girls began doing *calisthenics*, or light exercises to music. College girls learned a newly invented game called basketball. Girls found they could be as competitive as they wanted to be.

Still, many people believed sports would cause women to become too "manly," so more ladylike activities such as tennis and horseback riding (sidesaddle, of course!) were considered best for girls.

Sports Strides

Long skirts and tight corsets kept women in what some people thought was their proper place—home. It was Amelia Bloomer's introduction of loose-legged pants that let women take some of their first strides in sports. In the 1890s, wearing new "bloomers," women jumped onto bicycles and took off, feeling the wind in their faces. Bicycling became one of the first athletic activities widely popular with women.

Big Leap

Soon female athletes were proving they could be champions. In the 1920 Olympic Games, swimmer Ethelda Bleibtrey became the first American woman to win a gold medal. She was followed by a 14-year-old springboard diver named Aileen Riggin, who also took home a gold. And in 1926, 19-year-old Gertrude Ederle became the first woman to swim the English Channel.

Over the decades, girls kept swimming and swinging tennis rackets. They picked up golf clubs, softballs, and baseballs, too. And they started skiing, running, and throwing javelins. They formed teams and their own leagues so they could compete against other women.

Even so, by the 1970s boys still had more choices of sports to play, better equipment, and nicer gyms. But in 1972, Congress voted to change that.

A new law stated that any school receiving money from the federal government could not discriminate on the basis of sex. This landmark legislation, called Title IX, meant that what the boys got, the girls got, too, both in the classroom and on the playing field.

Title IX made a difference: In 1970, before the law was passed, 294,000 high school girls played sports. By 1978, that number was up to 1,600,000. In 1997, more than 2.4 million girls were playing high school sports.

Girl athletes today still fight stereotypes and discrimination. But they know that running fast and playing hard don't make you a tomboy. Girls today know that playing sports makes you healthy, strong, and confident.

So play what you want, against boys or girls. Race. Dive. Swim. Skate. Have fun!

Be Prepared!

Play it safe by heading to each practice and game prepared for success. Following these safety tips can help you get the most out of your performance and prevent injury.

Play It Simple

Remove necklaces, bracelets, earrings, and rings before you take the field. Anything that dangles can be dangerous. In many leagues, if you're caught wearing jewelry—even by mistake—you're disqualified. It's always safer to leave your fashion accessories at home.

Drink Up

Don't forget your water bottle! Sweating is your body's way of staying cool. If you don't replace the fluids you've lost through sweat, you'll become dehydrated—and that can affect your coordination and staying power.

Take several long drinks of water an hour before you exercise. During the game, take a drink every 20 minutes, whether you're thirsty or not. More thirst quenching after the game will help your body recover faster.

Protect Yourself

Wear your safety gear. Many sports require protective equipment like helmets, goggles, shin guards, pads, and mouth guards. Make sure you wear what's required, and make sure it fits. Last season's gear does little good if you've grown three inches since then. Ask a parent or coach to check the fit.

Dress for Success

In cold weather, wear layers of clothing that can be peeled off as your body warms up. In hot weather, light colors will keep you cooler. Your shoes don't have to be the most expensive brand in the store, but make sure they fit and are right for your sport. If you're not sure, ask your coach.

Get Ready!

Before you jump full-speed into practice or a game, your body needs time to get ready. Start out on the right foot by following a proper warm-up routine before exercising.

Warm Up

Five minutes of gentle activity raises your heart rate and gives your muscles a chance to get loose and ready to move. Try jogging in place or jumping rope. Get your heart rate going, but stop before you get out of breath.

Stre-e-e-tch Out

Ten minutes of stretching loosens up the muscles you'll be using during the game. The best stretching program covers all your major muscle groups. Ask your coach for a stretching routine that pays special attention to the muscles you use most in your sport. Your body is even more flexible after exercising, so stretch again when you're finished playing.

THE VALUE OF STRETCH

Go Team!

Teamwork
is spelled
with two
letters:

we.

All for One

You've seen the movie: The team is a bunch of misfits who bump into one another at every turn. Slowly, they get better, and at the end—big hurray—they bring home the trophy.

In real life, teammates don't go from chumps to champs in two hours. Teamwork takes time.

That's what practices are all about. They are a time to improve your own skills, to learn how to work with teammates, and to get to know one another. The more comfortable you feel with your teammates, the easier it is to play as one smooth machine.

How well do you know your teammates? Look at the girl next to you at practice. Who's her favorite pro player? What's her favorite sport? What's her dog's name? If you don't know, find out!

Once your teammates become friends, you develop a powerful closeness called *esprit de corps (es-PREE deh KOR)*. It's the spirit that makes working hard fun and that binds you together closerthanthis!

Getting to Know You

Play this quick game on the way to a meet, before practice, or while you wait for your ride home. It's a great way to build team unity.

1. This game is based on the rhythm in "A! My name is Anna, and I come from Alabama." Choose someone to begin. She says her name, then names her favorite athlete. *"J! My name is Jenna, and I like Mia Hamm."*

2. The next person says her own name and favorite athlete, then repeats the previous introduction. *"M! My name's Michelle, and I like Summer Sanders. J! Her name is Jenna, and she likes Mia Hamm."*

3. Continue around the group, with each person adding her own name and repeating the names that have come before. See how far you get without making a mistake! If someone goofs up, she starts the game over, beginning with her own name.

Team Effort

Teams are made up of all kinds of people—girls and boys, speed demons and slowpokes, girls with experience and girls who are just learning the game. Try to forget your differences and focus on what you have in common.

The best athletes know that being part of the team is more important than being the star of the show. You won't always get to play the position you want or be in the spotlight. So find your place on the team and learn to play your part well.

Being a team player doesn't mean abandoning your own goals. Dream big dreams! If you have your heart set on being the basketball team's starting forward, figure out how to get there. Write down your goals, and come up with a plan for achieving them. Where do you need to improve?

Work on being the best athlete you can be. But remember: you need your team in order to reach your goals. You're in this together.

"Your team is only as good as your weakest link, so you have to help that weakest link improve."
Kristin

Bad News Bears

Teamwork doesn't come easily. All those girls! All those personalities! Learning to spot bad behavior can help you stop trouble before it starts.

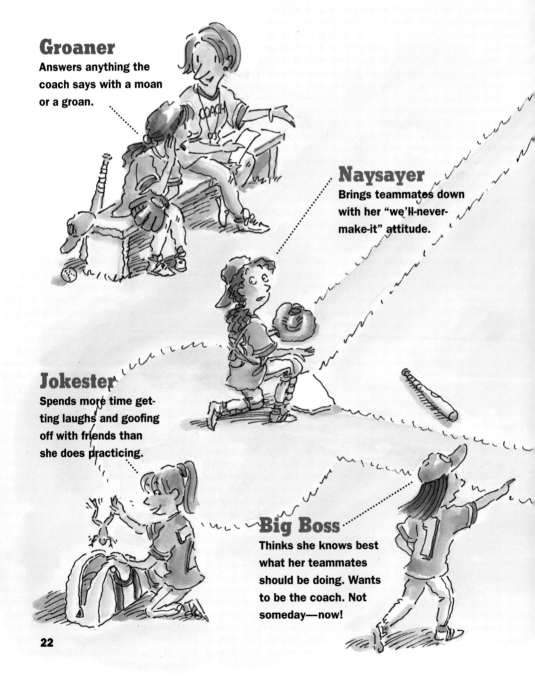

Groaner
Answers anything the coach says with a moan or a groan.

Naysayer
Brings teammates down with her "we'll-never-make-it" attitude.

Jokester
Spends more time getting laughs and goofing off with friends than she does practicing.

Big Boss
Thinks she knows best what her teammates should be doing. Wants to be the coach. Not someday—now!

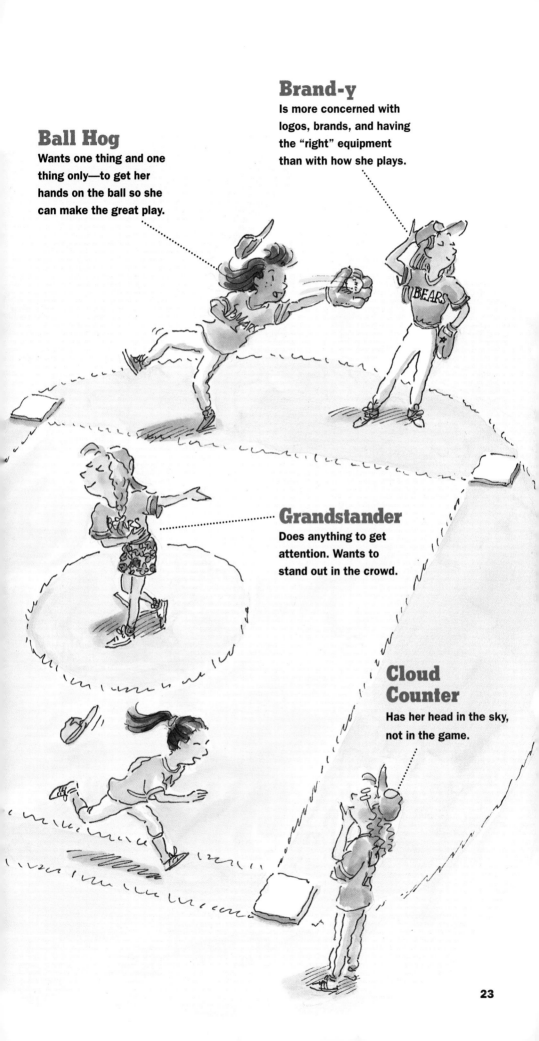

Ball Hog
Wants one thing and one thing only—to get her hands on the ball so she can make the great play.

Brand-y
Is more concerned with logos, brands, and having the "right" equipment than with how she plays.

Grandstander
Does anything to get attention. Wants to stand out in the crowd.

Cloud Counter
Has her head in the sky, not in the game.

The All-Stars

The most talented player isn't the only leader on the team. There are other ways to show award-winning behavior. Do you recognize any of these players?

Researcher
Loves to share information about new plays, training practices, and other ideas.

Energizer
Keeps team spirits high with her energy and encouragement.

Most Improved
Is living proof that hard work and practice do pay off.

Helper
Shares what she knows with other girls—without making them feel dumb.

Peacemaker
Smooths over disagreements and calms people down.

Extra-Effort Maker
Works hard at practice and really pays attention. Always ready to run one more lap.

Julie Foudy

As cocaptain and ten-year veteran of the U.S. Women's National Soccer Team, Julie Foudy knows a lot about the importance of keeping team relationships working.

"The strength of the national team," says Julie Foudy, "is that we're always fighting for each other on the field."

Have you ever gotten **mad** at a teammate because she made a **mistake?** What if you don't get along with someone on your team?

"I think many technical mistakes happen because a player lacks confidence. If you hammer a teammate when she makes a mistake, she'll doubt herself even more. The most constructive way I've found to handle it is to provide encouragement. If someone makes a technical mistake, I'll say, 'It's all right. Don't worry about it.'

"If someone makes a mistake because she's not hustling, that's sinful. I'll be a little harder. I might say, 'Come on. We need you to work harder for us.' It still doesn't have to be negative. You can put a positive spin on it.

"It's important to work out problems between people. There has to be a bond between teammates. On the national team, one of our greatest strengths is that we're such close friends. You might not think a problem between players is going to affect you, but it will. It will hurt the whole team."

Hey, Coach

"My favorite coach challenges us to learn. He doesn't let us become slackers."

Alexandra

Coaches can be friendly and funny, but tough, too. That's their job. Think of the best coach you've ever had. What made him or her great? The coach probably made you work hard at practice but also made the work seem fun. With the coach's help, you discovered skills you didn't know you had!

A coach's job is to help you become a better athlete. When a coach corrects you or gives you advice, don't take it as a personal insult. Coaches are there to teach you the rules of the game and help you develop the skills you need. That way, you're smart, strong, and ready to play when you take the field.

Can a coach be too tough? In some cases, yes. If your coach insults players or is verbally or physically abusive, tell a parent. Ask your parent to watch practice or a game and evaluate the coach. If enough parents think there's a problem, they can talk to the school or the head of the league. Don't be afraid to speak up.

Talk It Out

If you have a problem—say, you feel you don't get enough playing time—talk to your coach. She can't help you if you don't speak up! These tips make talking it out easier.

Go One-on-One

Approach the coach when she has time to think about what you're saying, not at a team meeting or in the middle of practice. Ask when she has time to discuss something important.

Go to the Coach First

Complaining to your teammates may make you feel better temporarily. But when griping gets back to the coach—and it always does!—it may make her less willing to hear you out later. Talk to the coach yourself instead of asking your teammates or parents to do it for you.

Calmly Explain How You Feel

Tears are not words. Whining and exploding are not the same as talking. Speak calmly, and give examples that support your point.

What not to say:

"You never let me play second base. You always make me play right field."

Better:

"My throwing has really gotten better and I've caught every ball that's come to me in the last three games. I'd like to try another position so I can get more experience."

The Coach Has the Final Word

If you don't like your coach's answer, ask for help. What can you do to improve? Ask if you can come up with a plan together that would get you where you want to go.

"But, Mom!"

If your father or mother coaches the team, you may get special attention—the good kind and the bad kind. Sometimes parents who coach give their daughters special favors. Other times they're extra hard on their own kids. Play it safe and don't look for special treatment. Ask Mom or Dad to treat you just as they treat the other players.

Huddle

Remember these truths about teammates:

Treat teammates as you'd like them to treat you. Give a compliment when someone plays well. It'll make you both feel good!

There's no "I" in the word team! Team players are as important as team stars. Everyone has a part to play.

Don't be afraid to talk to the coach if you have a concern. Tell her how you feel. The calmer and clearer you are, the easier it will be for the coach to help.

Always remember: A team is a powerful thing. Separately, each teammate can lift a tiny weight. Together you can move mountains.

Game
Time

when you believe, you achieve.

Get Set, GO!

The competition's just about to begin, and your body feels a rush of jumbled emotions. Your heart races. Your stomach flutters.

Those nervous, eager feelings are a good thing. They come from a substance called *adrenaline* that pumps through your body. Before a game, your body is a little like a can of soda that's been shaken up. The adrenaline is bubbling around inside you, making you feel nervous and edgy. When you start to play, that energy is released, like the liquid that fizzes out of the can when you pop it open.

You can keep jitters under control by learning to concentrate before a game and staying focused in the thick of it. Some people call it being "mentally tough." Some call it "putting on your game face." The key is to block out all distractions and focus on playing the best you can at that moment.

You know you're prepared. You can handle anyone who comes your way. Your body is saying you're ready to move. You've got the power. Use it.

Fight or Flight

A funny thing happens when you get into an exciting or stressful sports situation. Your body doesn't know if you are about to run a race or be run over by stampeding elephants. It just knows you're feeling anxious and gets you ready to take the challenge —or to take off.

Here's how this fight-or-flight response generally happens: Your brain tells the adrenal glands (located on the top of your kidneys) to release adrenaline into your blood. Adrenaline is the chemical that produces the changes your body needs to react. It makes your heart beat faster to pump more blood to the large muscles. It also sends fat and sugar into your bloodstream as sources of quick energy. These are all normal changes that get your body ready to move!

Chase Butterflies

Chase those butterflies out of your stomach so nerves don't get the best of you. Try these tricks to stay calm before—and during—the big event.

Take a Bird's-Eye View

Before the event, close your eyes and visualize a bird's-eye view of your performance. Imagine making all the moves you've practiced and see yourself playing your best. It's like watching a highlight film starring you!

Think Like a Fox

Be smart! Instead of worrying about how good your opponents are, think of one strength that you have that balances your opponents' strength. For example, they may be bigger, but you're quicker! Remember that even a simple strategy is better than no plan at all.

Remove the Rabbit Ears

Athletes who have "rabbit ears" listen too closely to the cheers and to the critics in the crowd. Don't let what other teams—or fans—say get to you. Ignore it and play your game.

Keep the Eye of the Tiger

Like a tiger, stay fierce and focused. Concentrate on doing the best you can at this very moment. Don't think about your false start in the last meet or whether you'll beat your best time. If you worry about what's happened in the past or what might happen in the future, you'll miss what's going on here and now.

Parent Traps

Most parents mean to be supportive when they attend their daughters' sporting events. But sometimes their words and actions send a different message.

Pressure Parents

Push their daughter to excel for all the wrong reasons: maybe because her sibling is a sports star or because it makes *them* look good. Either way, their win-or-die attitude saps the fun right out of the game.

Mr. Brag

Gloats constantly about his daughter's talent to other parents, the coach, teammates, and anyone else who will listen.

Go, Sally! You're the BEST!

Queen Mother

Treats her daughter as if she's better than everyone else. Cheers only for her own child instead of supporting the whole team.

No-Show Parents

May have many good reasons for missing almost every game—but it still hurts.

Loudmouths

Are certain *their* opinion is the right one. They argue with the officials, criticize the coach, and yell at the other team.

The Dark Clouds

As far as they are concerned, everyone's up to no good. The coach doesn't understand the game, the officials are blind, the school hasn't taken care of the field, and the team's in no shape to play.

Are You a Good Loser?

There's no disgrace in losing—it's a natural part of sports. But remember: not every loser is a sore one. What would you do in the following situations? Tell the truth!

1. You're very upset after your softball team loses. After the game, you say to the coach, "Why didn't you let me pitch? You know I could've done better than Emma. You never let me play where I can do some good for this team."

a. Yes, that's me.

b. I might do this.

c. I'd never do this.

2. You know you're a better swimmer than the girl who just beat you. But she had a better start. You lean over the rope, shake the winner's hand, and say, "Congratulations, but I would have won if I'd had a quicker start."

a. Yes, that's me.

b. I might do this.

c. I'd never do this.

3. Your team just lost a tough soccer match against opponents who played really rough ball. You and your teammate Maria saw them commit some nasty fouls that the official missed. You're supposed to shake hands with your opponents after the game, but Maria refuses. You stick with her. "She's right," you say. "We shouldn't have to be nice to cheaters."

a. Yes, that's me.

b. I might do this.

c. I'd never do this.

SCOREBOARD

Sore Loser

If you answered two or more **a**s, you sometimes push blame onto other people and dwell on negative thoughts, and that doesn't help you or your team. Look ahead to your next game and focus on what you can do to play your best.

Crossing the Line

If you answered mostly **b**s, you know in your heart what's right. Focusing on what teammates did wrong—or bursting the winner's bubble—may take away the sting a teensy bit, but it isn't O.K. Follow your conscience.

The Winner's Circle

If you answered mostly **c**s, you have the heart of a winner even when you lose. Teammates who've made mistakes know what they've done wrong, so why make them feel worse? A loss is already history. It's in the past, and there's nothing you can do about it. Keeping a positive attitude will help you start the next game right.

4. Your teammate missed a basket at the buzzer that would have won the game. Afterward, you say to her, "Looks like you need to practice your layups more, Dana." It's good advice, you think. After all, she shouldn't have missed that easy shot.

a. Yes, that's me.

b. I might do this.

c. I'd never do this.

5. Your hockey team has lost the first three games this season. The most recent loss really hurt—you thought for sure you'd beat the Purple Pythons. *If we didn't beat that team,* you think, *we're not going to beat anyone. This season will be awful.*

a. Yes, that's me.

b. I might think this.

c. I'd never think this.

Are You a Good Winner?

Are you as good in victory as you are in defeat? It's not always easy to be a graceful winner. What would you do in these situations?

1. Your team is way ahead. You're on the bench, waiting to go to bat. What do you do?

a. Relax. You've got it made and want to let the other team know it! Anyone want to have a bubble-blowing contest?

b. Get nervous. What if your teammate strikes out and starts the team on a downward slide? What if you're the only one who doesn't get a hit?

c. Stay focused. The game's not over yet. If your team gets too full of itself, your opponents might get mad enough to come from behind and win!

2. At the track meet, you and three teammates win all the relays. The four of you take the top places in almost every race, and your school wins. As you get on the bus with the rest of the team, you say:

a. "Ta-daa! Here we are—the four-girl track team."

b. Nothing. You just smile and look for a seat.

c. "Good job, everybody! Way to work together."

3. Your team wins the game with a basket right as the buzzer sounds. You:

a. Screech over and over at the top of your lungs, "Who's the best of all the rest? Yaaaaay us!"

b. Congratulate your teammates, find your parents, and go home.

c. Walk over to the other team and say, "Nice game. Your team is really good. Great job."

4. Your teammate's had a rough day. She made some mistakes that almost cost your team the game. Afterward, you:

a. Stay away from her. You don't want that bad luck rubbing off on you.

b. Talk to her but don't say anything about how she played. You don't want her to think about it.

c. Say, "It's O.K. Everybody makes mistakes. You're a good player, and this team needs you."

SCOREBOARD

Too Proud and Too Loud

If you answered mostly **a**s, you may come on too strong when you win. Don't let pride in a job well done turn to arrogance. Think twice before you gloat about a victory or ignore a troubled teammate.

Nothing Ventured, Nothing Gained

If you answered mostly **b**s, you could give just a little more heart. Show more team spirit. Praise a teammate—or a competitor—who has played well. Lend an ear to someone who's had a bad day. The good you give to others may come back to you.

Way to Go

If you answered mostly **c**s, you're on the right track. You know not to get cocky when your team takes a lead. You share victories with your teammates rather than hog the glory. You always congratulate the other team, win or lose. High five!

Nikki McCray

Nikki McCray and Cheryl Swoopes became friends when they played on the gold-medal 1996 Olympic basketball team. Here's what Nikki has to say about her friend becoming her opponent in the WNBA.

Does competing against a friend hurt your relationship?

"I always look forward to competing against a friend like Cheryl. Before the game starts, I go out and talk to her, give her a hug. There are no bad feelings. We know each other's strengths, and I want her to have a good game.

"Afterward, we steer away from talking about the game. We may go out to eat, but we talk about our family and friends. We leave the competition on the court."

When you play against a friend, Nikki says, remember that the game isn't about just the two of you. It's about your teams.

"When you're on the court, you have to separate yourself from the friendship. Don't think, *This is my friend.* Instead, think, *This girl is really good, and I have to go out and do what's best for my team to win.*

"Try not to compare yourself to your friend, either. You can't control whether or not your friend will play better than you. All you can control is how well you play.

"Focus on your own strengths, and everything else will fall into place."

She Said, He Said

What should you know if you're playing sports with boys—or against them? How do boys feel about playing against girls? Here are both sides of the story.

The Girls

"Sometimes I play basketball with boys. They give you tough competition, but I don't mind. That's how you get better."

Brittnee

"I've learned that boys are very aggressive. My advice is if you're playing with bigger boys, try to be just as aggressive and energetic as they are. If you aren't, they'll just walk all over you."

Krystal

"A lot of times when I play sports with boys, they pick out who they are going to throw the ball to and hog it between themselves. I'd rather play on an all-girl team."

Heather

"Don't think that just because you're a girl, you aren't good enough. More than likely, there will be a boy or two on the team who is not as good as you."

Lorilee

The Boys

"Boys should give girls a chance. Cooperate and give them the ball. Some girls might be better than boys. Boys can learn something from them!"

Brandon

"I have done coed soccer, swimming, track, and baseball. I would rather play on an all-boy team because sometimes girls talk too much."

Patrick

"I like playing on boy-girl sports teams because I think girls are less macho and less annoying. Girls who play on mixed teams should just be themselves and not be scared of bigger boys."

Madhan

"I like coed teams because I get to see the game from another point of view. In soccer I learned that some girls are faster and can kick farther than some boys. Sometimes, though, girls would get intimidated by boys and wouldn't try as hard to go for the ball. Girls should not be intimidated by boys who are bigger or stronger than them, because they might not be better."

Joe

You Say

If you get teased:

If someone tells you girls are no good at sports, tell them they're just plain wrong. Girls all over the world are running, throwing, and jumping—and they're *good.* If someone says you play like a girl, say, "I *am* a girl. So are the women on the Olympic hockey team, and they won a gold medal in 1998." If they call you a tomboy, tell them, "Nope. I'm a strong girl who likes to play sports."

If boys won't let you play or join their team:

Don't accept it. Say, "Come on, you know that's wrong!" If you can, just join in. If they still won't let you play, talk to individual boys from the group afterward. There may be only one or two who want to keep you out. If you can win a few people over, they may stick up for you the next day, when you go back to try again.

Survey Says

Would you rather play on an all-girl team or compete with—and against—boys? That's what *American Girl* magazine asked its readers. The results? The majority of girls who responded would rather play on all-girl teams. But the race was close:

1,456 voted to play on all-girl teams.

1,025 voted to play on girl-boy teams.

Luckily, the choice is usually yours!

Huddle

Get a grip on competition. Remember:

It's O.K. to be nervous. Once you get in the game and focus on the action, nerves usually disappear.

If your parents cause problems, tell them how you feel. It's worth working it out and having them there to cheer you on.

A good winner doesn't let glory go to her head. A good loser strives for a positive attitude, even when things don't go her way.

Facing a friend on the field? You are doing your friend a favor by playing your best against her. That way she gets to be her best, too.

Don't be intimidated by boys. Let your actions do the talking. Practice hard. Play like you mean it. That will earn you respect.

Crunch
Time

Success comes
in **cans.**
Failure comes
in can'ts.

Staying Strong

The good news: There will be times during the season when everything's going right. You're doing well and you feel *on*. Nothing can stop you.

The bad news: Other times, you will make mistakes—some little, some big. You may have a string of performances where nothing goes right. Or it may seem as if the refs are out to get you. At such times, it seems there's no way to get ahead.

You can't always avoid making mistakes. Nobody can. But how you react when you're down can determine whether you're a winner or a whiner.

Truth is, sometimes you may be stopping yourself. When things aren't going your way, do you see chances to shine—or to fail? If you realize you've been viewing the world through gloomy glasses, you have an advantage: you can take them off!

"When I tripped myself during a basketball game, I felt stupid. I recovered by stealing the ball and then making the shot."

Brittnee

Mind Power

Your brain is a powerful thing. The thoughts you have during a game can affect how well you play—especially if you make a onetime mistake seem like a big-time problem. Try these techniques for getting over goof-ups and errors.

Fire the Scorekeeper

Is there a little voice in your head keeping track of everything you do wrong? That's the slip-up scorekeeper getting in your way. Fire her! Instead, at the end of a game, congratulate yourself on five specific things you did well.

Close the Drawer

Imagine a tall dresser with many drawers. When you make a mistake, open a drawer, toss in the mistake, and close the drawer tight. You can't see the mistake anymore. It can't affect you, and it definitely doesn't determine how you'll play in the rest of the game. Lock the drawer and throw away the key!

Be Tough

Did you make a mistake because the other team was pushing you around? Your opponents know they stand a better chance of winning if they upset you. They want you to focus more on them than on the game. If you refuse to get upset or intimidated, you take away their power.

Breaking a Slump

Don't let simple screwups drive you to a down-in-the-dump slump. If mistakes keep getting in your way, ask yourself these questions. There may be some solutions to your problems close at hand.

Get Fit

Do you make mistakes because you're tired? You may need to work on *endurance,* your ability to stay strong through the end of the game. Ask your coach for training tips to build up your stamina.

Strategy Session

Do you keep making the same error? The problem may be that you're unsure what moves to make in certain game situations. Ask your coach for a private strategy session.

Technical Trouble?

Did you change any part of your technique before the slump started? Your new form may be throwing you off. Ask your coach to take a look at your technique.

Full Speed Ahead

Are you worrying too much about mistakes? When you goof up, it may feel as if time stops and all eyes are on you. In reality, the game doesn't slow down, so don't let your brain put on the brakes, either! Leave the mistake behind you. Put yourself back in the action, and focus on what's happening in the game right now.

"A champion isn't someone who never loses or falls down. It's someone who gets back up," says Michelle.

Michelle Kwan

The spotlight's been on skater Michelle Kwan when she's been at her highest heights—and lowest lows. Michelle has proven she can come back from disappointment stronger than ever.

How do you keep your hopes alive when your dreams don't play out as you've planned?

"In 1997, when I lost my titles at the National and World Championships, I was pretty upset at first," says Michelle. "It seemed that my worst fears had come true.

"I discovered I was so busy worrying about losing my titles that skating was becoming work to me, not the activity I love most in life, as it once had been.

"I came to the conclusion that whether I win or lose is never an important issue to me. Skating my very best and having fun doing it is the only thing that

matters. Being a champion takes drive, dedication, and practice, practice, practice! It's not worth it unless you really enjoy what you are doing."

Take Charge!

Only you control how well you play. It doesn't matter if the weather is sunny or dreary. It doesn't matter if your parents are there or if the crowd's on your side. If you let outside factors like these affect your performance, you're giving away control. It's as if you're riding a bike but letting someone grab the handlebars and steer you thisaway and thataway.

You can take charge of your thoughts! Try this quiz to see if you're in the driver's seat.

1. During games, I don't dwell on what my teammates might think of my moves.
a. That's me.   **b.** That's not me.

2. I know my parents will be happy with me even if I make a few mistakes.
a. That's me.   **b.** That's not me.

3. If an official gives me a bad call, I don't let it bother me during the entire game. I shake it off.
a. That's me.   **b.** That's not me.

4. I'm just as calm playing in front of a big crowd as when no one is watching.
a. That's me.   **b.** That's not me.

5. It doesn't matter if the other team has a good record. Every game is a fresh chance to prove myself.
a. That's me.   **b.** That's not me.

SCOREBOARD

In the Driver's Seat

If you had more "That's me" answers, you know that how well you play depends on *you* and how hard you try. You don't let other people's expectations get you down. You roll with the punches when something bad happens. Good going!

Time to Take Charge!

If you had more "That's not me" answers, remember that outside events don't affect how well you play unless you let them. During the game, concentrate on what you're doing while you're doing it. Forget what other people think or how the crowd is reacting. If an official's call goes against you, don't dwell on it. Focus on what you *can* do: play your best!

Power Drills

ant to be faster on your feet? Or known as the quickest hands in town? Give these skill drills a try. With a little practice, you'll reach your goals in no time!

Jump Start

Jumping rope works your lower and upper body, plus helps your coordination. When you can jump for 4 minutes straight, try the drills on pages 64 and 65.

1. Start out jumping for 2 minutes and 15 seconds using a 2-footed bounce.

2. Gradually work your way up to 4 minutes.

Popcorn Ball

This drill helps develop hand-eye coordination. Be sure to play outdoors or in an open gym where there's plenty of room. Once you get going, the ball will be bouncing like a crazy popcorn kernel!

The key is to keep your eyes on the ball. Watch it all the way into your hand as you catch it. After practicing Popcorn Ball, you'll be better at throwing and catching with both hands.

1. Stand 6 to 7 feet away from a wall. With your right hand, toss a tennis ball overhand at a spot on the wall a few feet above your head. Let the ball bounce back, and catch it with your left hand.

2. Without switching hands, throw the ball again, this time catching it with your right hand. Repeat, continuing to throw and catch with alternating hands.

The Plus Sign

This drill helps develop quickness and jumping ability. It can be done indoors on a gym floor or outdoors on a dry, hard-surfaced driveway or playground. Do this drill regularly, and have a friend time you. If you record the number of jumps you do each time, you can watch your speed improve!

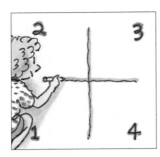

1. If you're outdoors, use chalk to draw a 4-foot-by-4-foot plus sign on the ground. If you're indoors, mark off the plus sign using masking tape.

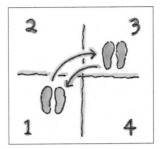

2. Begin with both feet in square 1. Jump diagonally to square 3 and back again. Repeat for 30 seconds. Count how many jumps you can do in that time.

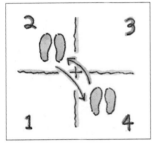

3. Rest for 30 seconds. Now switch to the other diagonal, jumping from square 4 to square 2 and back. Repeat for 30 seconds. How does your speed on each side compare?

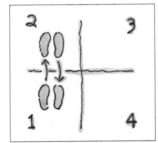

4. Rest for 30 seconds. Next, jump from square 1 straight up to square 2 and back. Repeat for 30 seconds. Count the number of jumps you can do, then rest for 30 seconds.

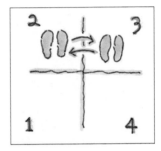

5. Jump from square 2 to square 3 and back for 30 seconds. Count your jumps and compare them to the other steps. In which direction do you jump the fastest? Keep working on your slower times, and they'll improve.

More Power Drills

Exercises that go from slow speed to high speed are great for building endurance. The pros call this *interval training*. The jump-rope drills below will help you last through even the longest games.

Bunny Hop

1. Start with 1 minute of steady, regular jumping. Use a 2-footed bounce, with both feet landing at the same time.

2. Without stopping, speed up for 15 seconds. Then slow down for 1 more minute. Repeat this sequence for 2 to 4 minutes.

Fast Forward

1. Skip or jog with the rope, one foot landing after the other. Jog 5 steps forward and 5 steps back. Continue for 1 minute.

2. Speed up your jump-rope jog for 15 seconds. Now go to a slow jog for 1 more minute. Repeat this sequence for 2 to 4 minutes.

Jumping Jack

1. On the first jump, land with both feet together. Keep your knees flexed and your weight on your toes.

2. On the next turn of the rope, spread your feet about shoulder-width apart. Repeat, alternating in and out, for 1 minute.

3. Speed up for 15 seconds, then slow down for 1 minute. Repeat for 2 to 4 minutes.

Skip n' Switch

1. On the first jump, land with both feet together.

2. On the next turn of the rope, land with the left foot slightly forward and the right foot back.

3. On the next jump, land with the feet together. ·

4. On the fourth jump, land with the left foot back and the right foot forward. Continue alternating forward-together-back-together for 1 minute.

5. Speed up for 15 seconds, then slow down for 1 minute. Repeat for 2 to 4 minutes.

Is It OK to Quit?

When you join a team, you make a commitment to your teammates, your coach, and yourself, so quitting is a big decision. Think it through. When is it all right to say "enough is enough"?

Teammate Troubles

I quit soccer because after I made a mistake in a game, my teammates ignored me for a month. They just wouldn't accept the fact that everybody makes mistakes. That's how we learn. After I quit soccer I joined a swim team (and I really like it).

Jenna

Too Busy

I decided to quit my junior golf team. I was so busy with other things that I couldn't devote 100 percent to golf. There were other girls good enough to be on the team, and I felt they deserved my spot.

Lorilee

Compromise

Two years ago I wanted to quit swimming. My parents would not let me because they said I needed to play a sport and be active. We worked it out so I could quit swimming in the spring and play softball instead.

Alexandra

Another Chance?

Last year I decided I wanted to quit swimming. I was having a pretty bad year, and I felt like I didn't want to swim again. But my parents made me do it again this year, and I am so happy they did. I look at swimming differently now. I think it's fun, and I love it.

Ashley

Final Word

Be sure to give the activity, your coach, and your teammates a fair shake. If the season is short, play until it's over and *then* decide. If the game's still not fun, it may not be the sport for you. Try something new next season and agree to give it your all.

Huddle

When things look bad, remember:

**In sports there are always peaks and valleys.
You can't learn without making mistakes.**

**Tough times teach you an important lesson:
that you can survive them.**

**Hardly anyone is born a "natural." Effort plus
practice determine how good you can become.**

**The way you think affects the way you play.
Keep a positive attitude, and you can make
your dreams come true.**

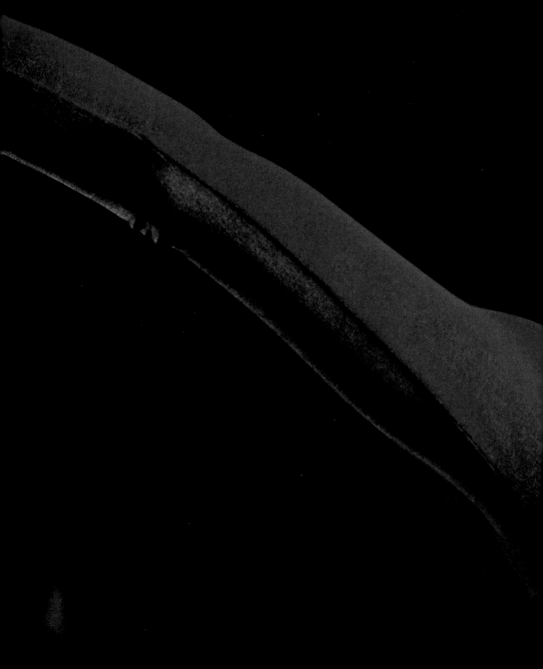

Getting
Serious

Success is sweet,
but its secret
ingredient is
sweat.

Bodyworks

Athletes ask a lot from their bodies. When you play sports, you have to pay special attention to eating right, so you stay strong.

Some girls think losing weight will enhance their performance. Girls in sports where they are graded by judges—figure skating, diving, gymnastics, and cheerleading—sometimes feel extra pressure to stay slim. Volleyball players, swimmers, and runners who wear revealing clothing may also become concerned about weight.

But the truth is, dropping pounds in an unhealthy way won't make you better. It will just make you weaker.

Calories are your body's fuel. The more you exercise, the more calories you burn. You need to replenish that fuel. Not eating enough or losing weight rapidly can lead to eating disorders, irregular menstrual cycles, and weak bones and muscles.

So if a coach or teammate is pressuring you to lose weight, talk to a parent. You can visit a doctor or nutritionist to check your weight and diet.

Don't pay attention to the numbers on the scale. Listen to how your body feels. When it comes to sports, strong is where you belong.

Eating Right

Good nutrition is important for all athletes, and especially for those who are spending more time and effort exercising. The best diet is a regular, balanced one that includes the foods shown below.

Training Table

If you're looking for a magic potion or a diet that will shoot you straight to the medal stand, you're out of luck. But some foods are better for you than others. Every day, young athletes need:

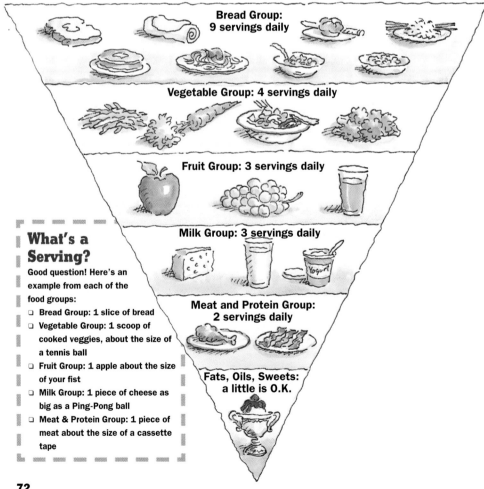

Bread Group: 9 servings daily

Vegetable Group: 4 servings daily

Fruit Group: 3 servings daily

Milk Group: 3 servings daily

Meat and Protein Group: 2 servings daily

Fats, Oils, Sweets: a little is O.K.

What's a Serving?

Good question! Here's an example from each of the food groups:

- ❏ Bread Group: 1 slice of bread
- ❏ Vegetable Group: 1 scoop of cooked veggies, about the size of a tennis ball
- ❏ Fruit Group: 1 apple about the size of your fist
- ❏ Milk Group: 1 piece of cheese as big as a Ping-Pong ball
- ❏ Meat & Protein Group: 1 piece of meat about the size of a cassette tape

Snack Right

After practice or a game, it's especially important to replace the energy you've used up. Carbohydrates, found in grain products and fruit, are one of the main sources of energy for working muscles. Try eating a low-fat, high-carbohydrate snack soon after exercising and another again two hours later. Some super snack ideas:

2 pieces of fruit

1 cup nonfat frozen or regular yogurt topped with blueberries

1 cup of grapes and 1 bagel

1 ounce cereal with ½ cup skim milk and ½ cup sliced banana

Drink Up

Where there's food, there must be drink! After exercise, you also need to replace the fluids you've lost through sweat. Try this fruity sports drink.

Slam Dunk

1½ cups raspberry-cranberry drink

¾ cup lemonade

Serve in a tall glass with ice. Add a lemon slice!

Kalyn Keller

Kalyn Keller, age 13, competes against top-notch swimmers from all over the world, including some famous athletes who've been her heroes. She's knows being a serious athlete means being strong mentally as well as physically.

In 1998, Kalyn took third in the 200-meter butterfly at the U.S.A. National Swimming Championships and was selected to represent the United States in the 1999 Pan-American Games in Canada. Next stop: Olympics 2000.

Is it **scary** to swim against older— even famous—athletes? How do you stay **motivated** for the six-days-a-week training regimen?

Kalyn trains all year, but during the competitive season she pushes herself even harder. She has two-hour work-outs twice a day on Mondays, Wednesdays, and Fridays, plus one two-hour session on Tuesdays and Thursdays.

"I used to get more nervous before really big meets," says Kalyn. "I was meeting swimmers like Janet Evans, Summer Sanders, and Brooke Bennett. They're Olympians!

"It was really neat to meet them and watch how they handled themselves. But when you get there, you have to make them not feel so big to you. Because if you're there, you're pretty much as good as they are. You have to realize that you belong there, too."

Kalyn admits her training is hard and that swimming at an elite level means she must make sacrifices. "I can't do much with friends from school and go places every weekend. But I still have fun," she says. "I try and remember what I want to do— go to the Olympics.

"My friends who don't swim don't understand why I do it. They think I can just swim fast. They don't know you *really* have to work on it."

Trainer's Tips

Sooner or later, almost every athlete encounters some kind of injury, big or small. Sports aches and pains fall into two basic categories: overuse injuries and acute injuries.

Overuse injuries happen when your body doesn't have the strength to withstand the same physical stress over and over again. These injuries often happen in sports like tennis and cross-country running. One common overuse injury is shin splints—shin pain sometimes caused by strong calf muscles pulling on weaker or less flexible shin muscles.

Acute injuries result from a sudden impact, like spraining your ankle after running into an opponent in a soccer game. When this happens, you can be out of the game for four to six weeks.

Sometimes a serious athlete's lifestyle makes her more prone to injury. Excessive stress—from balancing a tough workout schedule with school or dealing with pressures of competition—can leave your body in less than prime shape to perform. And that could lead to injury. If you find yourself frequently irritable, unable to sleep, and doing poorly in school, you may need to take a break.

If you do get injured, don't give up. Keep your head in the game, even if your body can't be. If you can't play, find another way to be valuable to your team. That way when your body heals, your mind will be ready to take the field.

To avoid injuries, try the training tips below. An extra bonus: they'll also help you go from a good athlete to a great one.

Start Right

Start the season in better shape by doing some off-season training. You can keep fit when you're not competing by just staying active. Running and bicycle riding are great off-season activities.

If you're not in top shape when the season begins, increase your workout gradually. Follow the 10% rule. Each week, increase your training time, the distance you cover, or repetitions of an exercise by just 10%. For example, if you start out by running 20 minutes each day, the next week you should run for 22 minutes.

Try Strength Training

Strength training is a form of exercise that increases your ability to push against or resist a force. Exercises that do this include sit-ups, pull-ups, push-ups, or a program *supervised by an adult* that uses free weights or weight machines. Research shows strength training can make your muscles stronger, help skills like sprinting and jumping, and decrease the risk of injury by making your tendons, ligaments, and bones stronger.

Stay Flexible

Tight muscles are more prone to injury. Stretching tight muscles during warm-up and cool-down sessions is especially important for growing athletes.

No Pain, No Gain?

Listen to your body. Sure, you have to work hard in sports. And that may mean sore muscles and minor aches here and there. But remember, pain means something. If you have mild to moderate pain for more than two weeks, see a doctor. If you have severe pain, get help immediately.

R.I.C.E. Advice

A sprained ankle is one of the most common sports injuries. If it happens to you, remember:

Rest Avoid using the sprained joint or putting weight on it.

Ice Apply an ice pack to help shrink swelling and ease the pain.

Compression Wrap the sprained area tightly in a stretchy Ace bandage to keep it stiff and to protect it from further injury.

Elevation Keep the sprained joint raised on a stack of pillows to help the swelling go down.

Stay off your ankle as much as possible. Apply an ice pack in 20-minute increments—20 minutes on, then 20 minutes off. While you're resting, elevate your ankle above the level of your heart. If that's not possible, elevate it at least six inches.

Huddle

Any girl who takes her sport seriously should know:

Keep your body fueled! Eat a healthy diet. Munch a high-carbohydrate, low-fat snack after exercise.

Drink up after you sweat it off! After practice or a game, be sure to replace your fluids with lots of water.

Believe in yourself. Stay strong mentally as well as physically.

Prevent injury by staying flexible and strong and practicing safely. If you feel pain, seek medical attention.

Team Spirit!

Sometimes **heart** is the strongest muscle of all.

Show Your Spirit!

Team togetherness can be powerful. It can be the secret weapon that gives your team strength and energy when you most need it.

But spirit is not just about seeing which team can scream the loudest. You can show your spirit in big ways and small. You might make a giant banner to hang at school on game day. Or you could write a special note to each teammate, telling her why she's important to the team. Showing your spirit makes playing sports more fun. That feeling you get is also what keeps you giving your all for the girls by your side—not just working against the other team.

Got Spirit? Let's Hear It!

Early in the Season
- Have a car wash to raise money—and to get to know your teammates

On Game Day
- Make posters to hang on your teammates' lockers
- Hang a sheet sign—a giant team poster painted on a white sheet
- Wear team T-shirts to school
- Try temporary tattoos

At the Game
- Sing a team song on the way there
- Tie on shoelaces in team colors
- Wear matching hair scrunchies

All the Time!
- Create a secret handshake
- Have a team motto—and use it
- Call teammates by special, positive nicknames

That's the Spirit

These girls have spirit, yes they do!
These girls have spirit, how about you?

Show Your Colors

We made team towels by dyeing them in our team colors. It was really fun!

Kaelan

Signs of Success

Two years ago, my softball team was the Ladybugs. My friend's mom and dad are artists and they made a big banner with our park and team name on it. We hung it at all our games.

Alexandra

Home Advantage

At our swim meets we put some of our pool water into the other team's pool. It makes us feel more like we're at home.

Gretchen

Cheer-io!

After every swim meet for the Sea Devils, we do this cheer so the other team knows we're good sports: *"Toothpaste, toothpaste, we use Crest. We think (other team's name) are the best!"*

Ashley

The More, the Merrier

My teams have done many different things to show team spirit over the years. Once I made about six posters for a one-day tournament. We've made cupcakes, worn body paint, glitter, colored hair spray, and lots more!

Kristin

Home of the Brave

Every athlete should know the words to the national anthem. Stand up, take off your hat, lay your hand on your heart, and sing along!

The Star-Spangled Banner

by Francis Scott Key

Oh, say, can you see,
by the dawn's early light,

What so proudly we hailed
at the twilight's last gleaming?

Whose broad stripes and bright stars,
thro' the perilous fight,

O'er the ramparts we watched,
were so gallantly streaming.

And the rocket's red glare,
the bombs bursting in air,

Gave proof through the night
that our flag was still there.

Oh, say, does that star-spangled
banner yet wave
O'er the land of the free
and the home of the brave?

Let's Celebrate!

Sharing rituals and special time with teammates gets you through defeats and makes victories even sweeter.

Team Tunnel

After soccer games—win or lose—all the parents make a tunnel for our team to run through.

Gretchen

Putt-Putt Party

We go miniature golfing at the end of the season. It's so much fun! I love hanging out with my team.

Ashley

Sweet Times

After a meet we have people over for ice cream or go to Dairy Queen. It's a celebration that tastes good!

Kaelan

Field Trip

My team went to a clinic together. The whole way there we sang Spice Girls songs. And we went shopping together and bought matching shirts.

Lorilee

Sports Center

The Sports Pages

Important Note
American Girl offers these Web site addresses as a source of information for you and your parents. We can't guarantee that these sites will give you the exact information you need, or that the addresses won't change after this book is printed. Always share information you get online with your parents, and never give out personal information.

Baseball
American Women's Baseball League
www.womenplayingbaseball.com
Promotes girls and women playing baseball around the world. Web site includes info on the league and its teams. On the Girl's Page, you can sign a petition to restart the All American Girls Professional Baseball League (featured in the movie *A League of Their Own*).

Little League Baseball
www.littleleague.org
Web site includes a kids' page, information on how to contact the league, plus pages on the league's World Series, summer camp, and museum.

Basketball
National Wheelchair Basketball Association
www.nwba.org
Web site includes info on kids' and adults' teams. Youth Division page includes photos, tournament information, and lists of clubs around the country.

Women's National Basketball Association
645 Fifth Avenue
New York, NY 10022
www.wnba.com
Web site includes news, features, schedules, and player profiles.

Cycling
U.S. Cycling Federation
One Olympic Plaza
Colorado Springs, CO 80909-5773
www.usacycling.org
Web site includes info on BMX racing, mountain biking, and road and track racing. Check out the Juniors Section for news on kids who bike.

Diving
U.S.A. Diving
Pan American Plaza
201 S. Capitol Avenue, Suite 430
Indianapolis, IN 46225
www.usdiving.org
Web site includes info on finding a diving club and news about the national and junior teams.

Equestrian Sports
Horsenet
www.horsenet.com
Web site is the home for horse lovers on the Internet. Includes info on dressage, vaulting, show jumping, and more.

U.S. Equestrian Team
Headquarters and Olympic Training Center
Pottersville Road
Gladstone, NJ 07934
www.uset.com
Web site includes biographies and history.

Fencing

U.S. Fencing Association
One Olympic Plaza
Colorado Springs, CO 80909-5773
www.usfa.org
Web site explains what fencing is, how
you can get involved, and more.

Field Hockey

U.S. Field Hockey Association
One Olympic Plaza
Colorado Springs, CO 80909-5773
www.usfieldhockey.com
Web site includes training information,
tips, and news.

Figure Skating

U.S. Figure Skating Association
20 First Street
Colorado Springs, CO 80906
www.usfsa.org
Web site includes biographies of U.S.
team members, articles from *Skating*
magazine, tips on finding a club near you,
and schedules of upcoming events.

International Figure Skating magazine
www.ifsmagazine.com
Web site includes articles from the cur-
rent issue and photo of the week.

Football

National Football League
280 Park Avenue
New York, NY 10017
www.nfl.com
See the kids' page for info on the annual
Punt, Pass & Kick competition, football
camp for kids, and more.

Golf

LPGA Girls Golf Club
www.lpga.com/junior/girls/girls.html
Web site includes info on finding a local
club in your state and news on other pro-
grams for kids.

Gymnastics and Rhythmic Gymnastics

U.S.A. Gymnastics
Pan American Plaza
201 S. Capitol Avenue, Suite 300
Indianapolis, IN 46225
www.usa-gymnastics.org
Web site includes a guide to artistic and
rhythmic gymnastics, articles, Team U.S.A.
news, and clubs near you.

Ice Hockey

U.S.A. Hockey
1775 Bob Johnson Drive
Colorado Springs, CO 80906-4090
www.usahockey.com
Web site includes info about how to join a
youth hockey program, training tips, and
national team news.

Jump Rope

U.S.A. Jump Rope Federation
P.O. Box 589
Huntsville, TX 77342
www.usajrf.org
Web site includes info on tournaments,
camps, workshops, and links to jump-
rope teams around the country.

Martial Arts

U.S.A. Karate Federation
1300 Kenmore Boulevard
Akron, OH 44313
www.usakarate.org

U.S. Judo Association
21 North Union Boulevard
Colorado Springs, CO 80909
www.csprings.com/usja

U.S. Taekwondo Union
One Olympic Plaza, Suite 405
Colorado Springs, CO 80909
www.ustu.com/

Orienteering

U.S. Orienteering Federation
P.O. Box 1444
Forest Park, GA 30298
www.us.orienteering.org
Web site answers the question "What is orienteering?" Tells how to use a compass and more.

Rock Climbing

Adventure Sports Online
www.adventuresports.com/asap/index/climbdir.htm
Web site bills itself as a resource for all kinds of outdoor adventure—from climbing to wilderness travel, backpacking, and water sports. The rock-climbing page features a glossary of terms, safety information, and lists of climbing gyms around the country.

Roller Skating

International Inline Skating Association
201 N. Front Street, #306
Wilmington, NC 28401
www.iisa.org
Web site includes tips for beginners, rules of the road, and info on places to skate.

U.S. Amateur Confederation of
Roller Skating
P.O. Box 6579
Lincoln, NE 68506
http://usacrs.com
Web site includes info on artistic skating, speed skating, roller hockey, the Roller Skating Museum, and joining a club.

Skiing and Snowboarding

The U.S. Ski Association
P.O. Box 100
Park City, UT 84060
www.usskiteam.com
Official Web site of the U.S. Skiing Association and the U.S. Ski and Snowboard teams. Info on alpine, cross-country, disabled, and freestyle skiing; ski jumping; and snowboarding.

Soccer

American Youth Soccer Organization
12501 South Isis Avenue
Hawthorne, CA 90250
www.soccer.org

Soccer Times
www.soccertimes.com
Web site includes info on youth soccer, the U.S. teams, World Cup, and college teams.

Softball

Amateur Softball Association
2801 NE 50th Street
Oklahoma City, OK 73111-7203
www.softball.org
The Web site of the national governing body for softball includes info on Junior Olympics and the Olympic women's team.

Women's Pro Softball League
90 Madison Street, Suite 200
Denver, CO 80206
www.prosoftball.com
Web site includes news on the league's six teams, game and TV schedules, and scores.

Speed Skating

U.S. Speedskating
P.O. Box 450639
Westlake, OH 44145
www.usspeedskating.org
Web site includes history of speed skating, news on U.S. team, and upcoming events.

Swimming

U.S.A. Swimming
One Olympic Plaza
Colorado Springs, CO 80909
www.usswim.org
Web site includes a kids' page, articles
on top swimmers, history, and how to find
swim clubs near you.

Synchro Swimming U.S.A.
Pan American Plaza
201 S. Capitol Avenue, Suite 901
Indianapolis, IN 46225
www.usasynchro.org
Web site includes photos, history, news,
scholarships, and articles on the Olympic
team.

Tennis

U.S. Tennis Association
70 West Red Oak Lane
White Plains, NY 10604
www.usta.com
Web site includes juniors page, U.S. Open
news, *Tennis* e-zine, and info on
wheelchair tennis.

Track and Field

U.S.A. Track & Field
1 RCA Dome, Suite 140
Indianapolis, IN 46225
www.usatf.org
Web site includes news of track stars
yesterday and today, tips, and info on Junior
Olympics and youth athletic championships.

Volleyball

U.S.A. Volleyball
715 S. Circle Drive
Colorado Springs, CO 80910
www.usavolleyball.org

Volleyball Worldwide
www.volleyball.org
Info for beginners to advanced players,
including skills tips, history, and rules. Links
to U.S. Youth Volleyball League, U.S.A.
Volleyball, and beach volleyball sites.

Water Skiing

U.S.A. Water Ski
799 Overlook Drive
Winter Haven, Florida 33884
www.awsa.com
Web site includes Kid's Club, Women of
WaterSports, info on summer camps and
ski schools, articles on top skiers, and
links to the Water Ski Hall of Fame.

Other

U.S. Association of Blind Athletes
33 N. Institute
Colorado Springs, CO 80903
www.usaba.org

U.S. Association for Disabled Athletes
143 California Avenue
Uniondale, NY 11553
Provides funds for disabled athletes.

Wheelchair Sports U.S.A.
3595 E. Fountain Boulevard, Suite L-1
Colorado Springs, CO 80910
www.wsusa.org/index.html

Nutrition

American Dietetic Association
216 West Jackson Boulevard, Suite 800
Chicago, IL 60606-6995
www.eatright.org

Organizations

Melpomene Institute
1010 University Avenue
St. Paul, MN 55104
www.melpomene.org
This nonprofit organization focuses on the
link between physical activity and health
for girls and women. Web site includes a
girls' page with sports-related games,
puzzles, and contests.

Tucker Center for Research on Girls
and Women in Sport
University of Minnesota
203 Cooke Hall
1900 University Avenue, SE
Minneapolis, MN 55455
www.kls.coled.umn.edu/crgws/news/
f96.html

Women and Girls in Sports
www.feminist.org/other/sports.html
Web site includes history of Title IX
legislation and articles on women in the
Olympics. Sponsored by the Feminist
Majority Foundation online.

Women's Sports Foundation
Eisenhower Park
East Meadow, NY 11554
www.womenssportsfoundation.org
Web site includes training tips, info on
National Girls and Women in Sports Day,
articles, and reports on important issues.

Olympics

U.S. Olympic Committee
One Olympic Plaza
Colorado Springs, CO 80909
www.usoc.org
Web site includes a kids' page, news on
athletes, and sports from A to Z.

Women in the Olympics
www.feminist.org/other/olympic/
intro.html
Celebrates 96 years of women in the
Olympics with profiles, history, and
photographs.

Online Magazines

Go, Girl! magazine—sports and fitness
for women
www.gogirlmag.com
News on sports, health, nutrition, and
fitness.

Just Sports for Women
www.justwomen.com/contents.html
News, scores, and advice for female
athletes and fans of women's sports.

Memory Pages

YOUR PICTURE

Record your sports goals, accomplishments and favorite moments.

I play all of these sports: ....

....

....

But ....
is my favorite sport to play.

The name(s) of my team(s):

My hardest game was when ....

....

....

....

From that I learned ....

....

....

....

....

....

My sports goal for this year is ....

....

....

....

....

Here are three steps I can take to achieve that goal:

1. ....

2. ....

3. ....

Three skills I can do better than last year are:

1. ....

2. ....

3. ....

My favorite sports memory is:

....

....

....

....

S
796
KAU

My most embarrassing moment in sports was when

My funniest moment was the time that

The most fun time my team had together was when

My favorite coach ever is

because

I have a good-luck tradition. It's

My big dream in sports is to

My favorite female athlete is:

place picture here

because

My favorite male athlete is:

place picture here

because